# You are ...

# From A to Z

## Who God Made
## You to Be

DAYNA MASON

Printed in the United States of America

First Printing: January 2019

International Standard Book Number-13: 9781795424264 (Softcover)

Visit the author's website at www.DaynaJo.com

# Dedication & Thanks

This book is dedicated to my magnificent daughter and my amazing son, who inspire me every day.

I would like to thank those who made this book possible. They were instrumental in helping me to move beyond my need to keep my spiritual life private and they were the catalyst for me being able to share the message of this book with you.

Thank you, Wil Mayfield, for helping release me from my self-imposed religious oppression. I am forever grateful. Thank you, Harvey Buck, for giving me the much-needed tools to dive deeper into the Bible for the meaning I knew was there all along. Thank you, Kerry LeBleu, for sharing your beautiful idea for this perfect little book. An idea that was exactly what I needed to give expression to the message I've wanted to communicate from the time I was twelve years old. Your generosity and inspiration will forever be appreciated.

# Introduction

You are an amazing original, created by God who loves you immeasurably. No one can take your place.

Use this book to remember the truth about who you are, the truth about who God made you to be.

You can read this book from the beginning to the end, or you can open it to any page and take in the message of that page.

Regardless of which approach you choose, the hope is that each page will remind you of how important you are to God and to this beautiful life.

*You are ...*

# *A*lways on

# God's mind.

God is always thinking about you. Always waiting for an invitation to participate in your life.

*"So God answers, "Can a mother forget her nursing baby and lack compassion for the child of her womb? Even if that were possible, I will never forget you. See, I have engraved you on the palms of my hands."*

*Isaiah 49:15-16*

# NOTES

*You are ...*

*B*orn with a purpose.

There is no one like you. Only *you* can fulfill God's loving intention for your life.

*"For I know the plans I have for you," declares God, "plans to prosper you and not to harm you, plans to give you hope and a future."*
                                                    *Jeremiah 29:11*

# NOTES

*You are ...*

*C*ared for.

You have nothing to fear. Give your worries to God because God takes care of you.

*"Cast all your anxiety on God because God cares for you."*

*1 Peter 5:7*

# NOTES

*You are ...*

# Daring.

You can take risks knowing that God will be with you every step of the way, giving you strength and courage, and catching you if you fall.

*"For nothing will be impossible with God."*
*Luke 1:37*

# NOTES

*You are ...*

# Enough.

You are complete. Right now. There is nothing you can do to improve on God's perfect design.

*"You are altogether beautiful, my love; there is no flaw in you."*

*Song of Solomon 4:7*

# NOTES

*You are ...*

# *F*ree.

Don't let the world tell you who you are. Let God show you the *truth* of who you are. Once you know the truth, you will be forever set free.

*"And you will know the truth, and the truth will set you free."*

*John 8:32*

# NOTES

_____
_____
_____
_____
_____
_____
_____
_____
_____
_____
_____
_____
_____
_____
_____
_____
_____
_____
_____
_____
_____
_____
_____

*You are ...*

# Gifted.

You have something uniquely you to give to the world. No one can do it like you. No one can do it for you. The world needs you.

*"You have been given unique gifts. Use them accordingly: If your gift is prophesying, then prophesy in accordance with your faith; if it is serving, then serve; if it is teaching, then teach; if it is to encourage, then give encouragement; if it is giving, then give generously; if it is to lead, do it diligently; if it is to show mercy, do it cheerfully."*

*Romans 12:6-8*

# NOTES

_____

_____

_____

_____

_____

_____

_____

_____

_____

_____

_____

_____

_____

_____

_____

_____

_____

_____

_____

_____

_____

_____

_____

_____

*You are ...*

*H*oly.

Distinguished. Sacred. Different. Set apart. You are in the world, but not of it. Because you are created in the likeness of God, your magnificence transcends the human experience.

*"You are holy because I am holy."*
1 Peter 1:16

# NOTES

*You are ...*

# *I*ntrinsically guided.

You are equipped with a heart guidance system. A *God compass*. When you follow God's navigation, your best outcome is realized.

*"Trust in God with all your heart and do not rely on what you think you know; Seek God's will in all you do, and God will show you which path to take."*

*Proverbs 3:5-6*

# NOTES

*You are ...*

# $\mathcal{J}$ust.

You give to others what they need, not necessarily what is equal. God's justice is equity not equality.

*"In everything, therefore, treat people the way you want them to treat you."*

*Matthew 7:12*

# NOTES

*You are ...*

# $\mathcal{K}$nown.

God *knows* every detail of your existence, inside and out. Your personality, your humanness, your joy, your grief, your aches and your desires. All of it. You are *known*.

*"God formed my inward parts; God knitted me together in my mother's womb. I am reverently and wonderfully made. Wonderful is God's workmanship; my soul knows very well."*
                                                        *Psalm 139:13-14*

# NOTES

*You are ...*

# *L*ove & Loved.

God is love, therefore you are love. Nothing can separate you from God's love, because you *are* God's love. When you express love, you expand that love into the world.

*"Neither height nor depth, nor anything else in all creation, will be able to separate you from the love of God."*

*Romans 8:39*

# NOTES

*You are ...*

# *My* delight.

Like a parent adores a child, God is delighted by you and wants to give you your heart's desires.

*"Find delight in God, and God will give you the desires of your heart."*

*Psalm 37:4*

# NOTES

_____

_____

_____

_____

_____

_____

_____

_____

_____

_____

_____

_____

_____

_____

_____

_____

_____

_____

_____

_____

_____

_____

_____

_____

_____

_____

_____

*You are ...*

*N*ot alone.

God is with you wherever you go. You cannot be apart from God because God is part of you.

*"Be strong and courageous. Do not be frightened or discouraged, for God is with you wherever you go."*

*Joshua 1:9*

# NOTES

*You are ...*

An Overcomer.

You can overcome any adversity. God provides you with peace to move through all circumstances free from suffering.

*"I have told you these things, so that in me you may have peace. In this world you will have distress. But have courage! I have overcome the world."*

*John 16:33*

# NOTES

*You are ...*

# $\mathcal{P}$owerful.

You are immeasurably powerful. When you liberate yourself from your fear, your presence automatically liberates others. God made you powerful and loving, not fearful.

*"For God gave us a spirit not of fear but of power and love and self-control."*
                                    *2 Timothy 1:7*

# NOTES

*You are ...*

# A Quintessential

# expression of God.

You are a creator. You cause things to happen.
You get to choose what imprint you want to
make on the world.

*"God created you in the likeness of God."*
                                   *Genesis 1:27*

# NOTES

*You are ...*

# Radiant light.

You are meant to shine, like children do. You are designed to express the radiance of God that is within you. As you let your light shine, others feel permission to do the same.

*"You are like light for the whole world. A city built on a hill cannot be hid. No one lights a lamp and puts it under a bowl; instead it is put on the lampstand, where it gives light for everyone in the house. In the same way your light must shine before people."*

*Matthew 5:14-16*

# NOTES

*You are ...*

# $S$till forgiven.

You are already forgiven. No matter what mistakes you make you are still forgiven. God has set you free from the power of shame. Forgive yourself and choose again.

*"God has rescued us from the power of darkness and has brought us into the kingdom of God, by whom we are set free, that is, our failures are forgiven."*

*Colossians 1:13-14*

# NOTES

*You are ...*

# $\mathcal{T}$ransformed.

You are empowered by God's transformation of your thoughts. Don't let the world tell you what's best for you. Follow God's perfect desire for your life.

*"Don't copy the behavior and customs of this world, but let God transform you by changing the way you think. Then you will learn to know God's desire for you, which is intrinsically good, gratifying, and complete."*

*Romans 12:2*

# NOTES

*You are ...*

# *U*nderstood.

God sees you and knows you better than you know yourself. God knows your heart and understands everything you think and do.

*"God doesn't see things the way you see them. People judge by outward appearance, but God looks at the heart."*

*Samuel 16:7*

# NOTES

*You are ...*

# $\mathcal{V}$alued.

You have a special place in God's heart reserved just for you. You are priceless and irreplaceable.

*"You have a special place in my heart."*
                                        *Philippians 1:7*

# NOTES

*You are ...*

# *W*orthy.

You are perfectly suited to do everything God leads you to do. You don't need to earn your standing in life. You are complete exactly the way you are.

*"I can do all things through God who strengthens me."*

*Philippians 4:13*

# NOTES

*You are* ...

# Xtraordinary.

You are a phenomenal work of art. Uniquely created. An inimitable masterpiece.

*"You are God's masterpiece."*

*Ephesians 2:10*

# NOTES

*You are ...*

# Young in heart.

Your heart is innocent. When you remember to look at life with childlike wonder, you experience the loving power of God.

*"Become like a child and you will experience the power of God."*

*Matthew 18:3-4*

# NOTES

*You are ...*

A *Z*oetic soul.

You are a vital spiritual human. Your being is where God's presence lives and breathes. Care for your body and mind with the same honor, respect, love and reverence that you would have for God's house.

*"Do you not know that you are God's temple and that God's Spirit dwells in you?"*

*1 Corinthians 3:16*

# NOTES

# About the Author

**Dayna (Reid) Mason**, Bestselling Author, Writer and Minister. She has officiated weddings for over 18 years. Her love for people and the desire to provide couples with a non-judgmental and personalized approach to selecting the words spoken at their wedding inspired her to seek ministry ordination.

Although Dayna personally believes in God, she also believes, "Everyone has to find their own way in this world, including any beliefs they may have about the mysteries. Because truly, all we really have is a faith in what we believe to be true."

**Other Books by Dayna (Reid) Mason:**

"**Do-It-Yourself Wedding Ceremony:**
Choosing the Perfect Words and
Officiating Your Unforgettable Day"

"**Do-It-Yourself Wedding Ceremony
Guidebook:** Choosing the Perfect Words
and Officiating Your Unforgettable Day"

"**Sacred Ceremony:** Create and Officiate
Personalized Ceremonies"

"**Funerals & Memorials:** Creating the
Perfect Service to Remember a Loved
One"

"**Officiating Weddings:** Start a Profitable
Business Marrying Couples"

"**Wedding Officiant Guidebook For
Beginners:** How to Become Ordained and
Perform a Marriage Ceremony Script"

"**I'm Just That Into Me:** You're the One
You've Been Waiting For"

23896400R00035

Made in the USA
San Bernardino, CA
04 February 2019